Four Huts

FOUR HUTS

Asian Writings on the Simple Life

Translated by Burton Watson
Illustrated by Stephen Addiss

SHAMBHALA
Boston & London
1994

Shambhala Publications, Inc.
Horticultural Hall
300 Massachusetts Avenue
Boston, Massachusetts 02115

9 8 7 6 5 4 3 2 1

First Edition
Printed in the United States of America on acid-free paper ♾
Distributed in the United States by Random House, Inc., and
in Canada by Random House of Canada Ltd

Library of Congress Cataloging-in-Publication Data

Four huts: Asian writings on the simple life/translated by
    Burton Watson: illustrated by Stephen Addiss.—1st ed.
        p.   cm.—(Shambhala centaur editions)
    Translation of poems by four classical Asian poets.
    ISBN 1-57062-001-6 (pbk. : alk. paper)
    1. Japanese literature—To 1868—Translations into
English. 2. Pai, Chü-i, 772–846—Translations into
English. I. Watson, Burton, 1925– . II. Addiss,
Stephen, 1935– . III. Series.
PL782.E1F68   1994   94-9608
895.6′1008—dc20   CIP

The Master said, "What a fine man Hui was!
One container of rice, one dipperful of drink, living in
a back alley—others couldn't have endured the gloom
of it, but Hui never let it affect his happiness.
What a fine man Hui was!"

—The Confucian Analects

Contents

Acknowledgments

The translation of the *Record of the Pond Pavilion* appeared earlier in *Japanese Literature in Chinese*, vol. 1 (New York: Columbia University Press, 1975). The translation of the *Record of the Hut of the Phantom Dwelling* appeared in *From the Country of Eight Islands*, tr. and ed. by Hiroaki Sato and Burton Watson (New York: Doubleday & Company, 1981). Both are presented here in slightly revised form with the permission of the publishers.

Translator's Preface

THE HOUSE AS a metaphor for the house-holder, or for the particular kind of life lived in it, is a very old idea and figures in the literature of many different countries and periods. In the four pieces translated here, four householders describe for us in some detail the house they are living in at the moment and the sort of life they live there. And through this medium they succeed in conveying, subtly and for the most part indirectly, their underlying sense of the world and what is to be valued in it.

All four are writers and poets, two of them very renowned poets, and all mention musical instruments or the pleasure they derive from music. One is Chinese, the other three are Japanese. One lives in a house that is rather grander than he would care to admit; the other three occupy what can only be described as huts. Two have a wife and family, two are life-long bachelors. All claim to be highly contented with their dwellings and say they hope to go on living in them, though not all of them do so. All are fervent followers of Buddhism, and two actually became monks in their later years. Two wrote in Chinese, two wrote in Japanese. All clearly took pains to clothe their accounts in the most elegant and effective language they could devise. The first wrote his piece in 817, the second in 982, the third in 1212, the fourth in 1690.

These four pieces are interesting first of all

for what they tell us about the physical surroundings in which these men lived, and about their mental and spiritual lives. Second, they are interesting as examples of how four different writers of great literary talent handled this particular type of descriptive piece: how much space they devoted to an objective account of their house and its setting and how much to their own thoughts and activities there. Two, for example, confined their accounts almost entirely to personal matters; the other two ranged further afield to relate various historical events.

Finally, the pieces are interesting as examples of literary influence. In the case of the first writer, the Chinese poet-official Po Chü-i, we cannot point to any specific work that served as a model for his description of his little house on Mount Lu, though descriptive pieces of this sort were common in the literature of the T'ang dynasty, the period in which he lived. The second writer, the Japanese government official Yoshishige no Yasutane, however, clearly patterned his work on the piece by Po Chü-i, and in it he mentioned Po by name. The third writer, the poet and musician Kamo no Chōmei, may or may not have been familiar with Po Chü-i's account, but there is no doubt that he knew and was deeply influenced by Yoshishige no Yasutane's. The haiku poet Matsuo Bashō, the last writer, was probably acquainted with all three of the earlier works translated here, though in his own work he chose to return to the terser form and the calmer, more optimistic tone of the first piece in the series, Po Chü-i's.

Thus, reading the four pieces in succession, we see how the different writers shaped the form to their individual needs and tastes, expanding certain themes, adding new ones, dropping others entirely. Certain ideas run through all the pieces—love of nature, poetry and music, simplicity, and the quiet life. Certain unspoken questions underlie them all—what constitutes happiness in this life, how should we pursue it, what are its minimum requirements?

Read in series, the pieces show how a literary idea can evolve and expand in the hands of a succession of writers. Taken as a whole, they give eloquent expression to one of the most important ideals in the artistic and spiritual life of China and Japan, that of the simple life lived in a simple dwelling.

Record of the Thatched Hall
on Mount Lu

Introduction

Po Chü-i, or Pai Chü-i, whose polite name was Lo-t'ien, was one of the most prolific and popular of the major T'ang poets. The son of an impoverished scholar-official, he passed the civil service examinations with distinction and was appointed to various government posts in and around the T'ang capital city of Ch'ang-an. In his poetry and official reports, however, he frequently spoke out against the government policies of the time. Eventually he was accused of overstepping his authority and in 815 was demoted to a lowly post as *ssu-ma* or marshal in the district administration of

Chiang-chou, a remote rural area south of the Yangtze River in present-day Kiangsu Province. He proceeded to the town of Chiu-chiang to take up his new post, and the following year he began making trips to nearby Mount Lu. As he relates in the following prose piece, he was so taken with the scenery there that he determined to build a little house on the mountain where he could stay when official duties did not detain him.

Mount Lu is an extensive complex of peaks and valleys, the site of numerous Buddhist and Taoist temples. Po was a devout Buddhist believer, and during his stays on the mountain he often went to the Buddhist temples to practice Zen-style meditation with the monks. Mount Lu is often referred to as Mount K'uang Lu because of a recluse of the surname K'uang who was said to have lived there in ancient times. Po called his house on the mountain a *ts'ao-t'ang* or "grass-thatched hall" in imitation of the house of that name where the famous poet Tu Fu (712–770) lived when he was in Ch'eng-tu.

The prose piece is in the *chi* or "record" form, a very common form in Chinese literature. In T'ang times it was used for descriptive pieces, particularly those that commemorate a journey or outing, a building, or a natural scene of unusual beauty. The works in *chi* form by Po Chü-i's contemporary Liu Tsung-yüan (773–819) depicting the scenes in his place of exile in the south are especially famous. Po Chü-i wrote a number of short prose works in the *chi* form.

At the end of the prose piece describing

Po's mountain home I have appended translations of two well-known poems by him that deal with his life there. Though Po expressed a desire to retire from official life entirely and live out the rest of his days in his mountain home, he was transferred to a post in another part of the country at the end of 818 and had to leave his thatched hall less than two years after it was completed.

Record of the Thatched Hall on Mount Lu

by Po Chü-i

K'UANG LU, so strange, so superb it tops all the mountains in the empire! The northern peak is called Incense Burner Peak, and the temple there is called the Temple of Bequeathed Love. Between the temple and the peak is an area of superlative scenery, the finest in all Mount Lu. In autumn of the eleventh year of the Yüan-ho era [816] I, Po Lo-t'ien of T'ai-yüan, saw it and fell in love with it. Like a traveler on a distant journey who passes by his old home, I felt so drawn to it I couldn't tear myself away. So on a site facing the peak and flanking the temple I set about building a grass-thatched hall.

By spring of the following year the thatched hall was finished. Three spans, a pair of pillars, two rooms, four windows—the dimensions and expenditures were all designed to fit my taste and means.[1] I put a door on the north side to let in cool breezes so as to fend off oppressive heat, made the southern rafters high to admit sunlight in case there should be times of severe cold. The beams were trimmed but left unpainted, the walls plastered but not given a final coat of white. I've used slabs of stone for paving and stairs, sheets of paper to cover the windows; and the bamboo blinds and hemp curtains are of a similar makeshift nature. Inside the hall are four wooden couches, two plain screens, one lacquered *ch'in*,[2] and some Confucian, Taoist, and Buddhist books, two or three of each kind.

And now that I have come to be master of the house, I gaze up at the mountains, bend down to listen to the spring, look around at the trees and bamboos, the clouds and rocks, busy with them every minute from sunup to evening. Let one of them beckon and I follow it in spirit, happy with my surroundings, at peace within. One night here and my body is at rest, two nights and my mind is content, and after three nights I'm in a state of utter calm and forgetfulness. I don't know why it's like this, but it is.

If I asked myself the reason, I might answer like this. In front of my house is an area of level ground measuring ten *chang* square.[3] In the middle is a flat terrace covering half the level ground. South of the terrace is a square pond twice the size of the terrace. The pond is surrounded by various types of indigenous bamboo and wildflowers, and in the pond are white lotuses and silvery fish. Continuing south, one comes to a rocky stream, its banks lined with old pines and cedars, some so big that ten men could barely reach around them, some I don't know how many hundred feet in height. Their upper limbs brush the clouds, their lower branches touch the water; they stick up like flags, spread like umbrellas, rush by like dragons or serpents. Under the pines are many clumps of bushes or thickets of vines and creepers, their leaves and tendrils so interwoven that they shut out the sun and moon and no light reaches the ground. Even in the

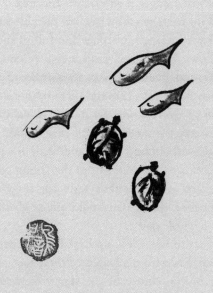

hottest days of summer the breeze here is like autumn. I have laid a path of white stones so that one can go in and out of the area.

Five paces north of my hall the cliff rises up in layers, heaped in stones and full of pits and hollows, bulges and projections. A jumble of trees and plants blanket it, a mass of dense green shade with here and there festoons of red fruit. I don't know what they're called, but they stay the same color all year round. There is also a bubbling spring and some tea plants. If you used the water from the spring to brew tea, and people with a taste for such things happened along, they could amuse themselves for a whole day.

East of the hall is a waterfall, the water tumbling down from a height of three feet, splashing by the corner of the stairs, then running off in a stone channel. In twilight and at dawn it's the color of white silk, and at night it makes a sound like jade pendants or a lute or harp.

The west side of the hall leans against the base of the northern cliff where it juts out to the west, and there I've rigged a trough of split bamboo to lead water from the spring in the cliff, carry it across to my hall, and divide the flow into little channels so that it falls from the eaves and wets the paving, a steady stream of strung pearls, a gentle mist like rain or dew, dripping down and soaking things or blowing far off in the wind.

On four sides these are the sights that meet my eyes and ears, that my shoes and walking stick take me to: in spring the blossoms of Brocade Valley, in summer the clouds of Stone

Gate Ravine, in autumn the moon over Tiger Creek, in winter the snows on Incense Burner Peak. Now sharply seen, now hidden, in clear or cloudy weather; concealed, revealed, in twilight or at dawn; undergoing a thousand changes, assuming ten thousand forms—I could never finish describing them or capturing them all in words. Therefore I say the scenery here is the finest in all of Mount Lu.

Ah, even an ordinary man, if he builds himself a house, fits it with bed and mat, and lives there awhile, can't help putting on an air of boastfulness and pride. And now here I am, master of a place like this, with all these objects offering me understanding, each after its own kind—how could I be anything but happy with my surroundings and at peace within, my body at rest, my mind content!

Long ago Hui-yung, Hui-yüan, Tsung Ping, Lei Tz'u-tsung, eighteen men in all, came to this mountain, grew old and died here without ever going home.[4] Though they lived a thousand years ago, I can understand what was in their hearts, because I'm here too.

What's more, when I think back, I see that from youth to old age, wherever I've lived, whether in a humble house or a vermilion-gated mansion, even if I stayed no more than a day or two, I immediately began dumping basketfuls of earth to build a terrace, gathering fist-sized stones for a miniature mountain, and damming up a few dippers of water to make a pond, so great is this weakness of mine, this fondness for landscapes!

Then one morning I met with trouble and demotion, and I came here to lend a hand in the administration of Chiang-chou. The magistrate of the district treated me with kindness and generosity, and Mount Lu was waiting for me with these superb sights and wonders! Heaven arranged the time for me, earth provided the place, and so in the end I've gotten what I like most. What more could I ask for?

But still I'm saddled with my post as a supernumerary official, and with other entanglements I can't get free of just now, so I come and go, not yet able to sit down and rest. Some day, though, when I've married off my younger siblings and served out my term as marshal, when I can stay or go as I choose, then you may be certain I'll take my wife and family in my left hand, gather up my *ch'in* and books in my right, and live out the remainder of my days here, fulfilling the wishes of a lifetime.

You clear spring, you white rocks, listen to what I say!

On the twenty-seventh day of the third month I moved into my new hall. On the ninth day of the fourth month, Yüan Chi-hsü of Ho-nan, Chang Yün-chung of Fan-yang, Chang Shen-chih of Nan-yang, and the priests Ts'ou, Lang, Man, Hui, and Chien of the East Forest and West Forest temples, twenty persons in all, joined me in a vegetarian meal, passing around tea and fruit to celebrate the completion of my hall.[5] At that time I wrote this Record of the Thatched Hall.

Two Poems on the Thatched Hall

BELOW Incense Burner Peak I built a new mountain dwelling. When my thatched hall was completed, I had occasion to inscribe this on the eastern wall.

A new thatched hall, five spans by three;
stone steps, cassia pillars, fence of plaited
    bamboo.
The south eaves catch the sun, warm on winter
    days;
a door to the north lets in breezes, cool in
    summer moonlight.

Cascades from the spring that drip on the
   paving splatter it with dots;
the slanting bamboo that brushes the window
   isn't planted in rows.
Next spring I'll thatch the side room to the
   east,
fit it with paper panels and reed blinds for my
   Meng Kuang.[6]

꙳

The sun's high, I've slept enough, still too lazy
   to get up;
in a little room, quilts piled on, I'm not afraid
   of the cold.
The bell of the Temple of Bequeathed
   Love—I prop up my pillow to listen;
snow on Incense Burner Peak—rolling up the
   blind, I look at it.

K'uang's Mount Lu, a place for running away
    from fame;
marshal—a fitting post to spend old age in.
Mind peaceful, body at rest, this is where I
    belong.
Why should I always think of Ch'ang-an as
    home?

NOTES

1. A span is the distance between two pillars or columns in a Chinese house. This seems to indicate that Po's hall had four columns to a side and was square. But in one of the poems quoted at the end of the prose piece he gives the dimensions as three spans by five. The two pillars are the supports for the ridgepole.

2. The *ch'in* is a zitherlike stringed instrument played in horizontal position.

3. One *chang* is ten Chinese feet.

4. Hui-yung (n.d.) and Hui-yüan (334–416) were eminent Buddhist priests who lived on Mount Lu, the former at the Hsi-lin-ssu or West Forest Temple, the latter at the Tung-lin-ssu or East Forest Temple. Tsung Ping (375–443) and Lei Tz'u-

tsung (386–448) were scholars who were followers of Hui-yüan and, along with a number of
other monks and laymen, participants in devo-
tional activities led by Hui-yüan.

5. Ts'ou is Shen-ts'ou of the Hsing-kuo-ssu Temple.
Man's full name is Chih-man, Chien's is Shih-
chien. Lang and Hui have not been identified.

6. Meng Kuang was the wife of Liang Hung, a recluse of the Later Han; the couple is regarded as
the epitome of conjugal happiness.

Record of the Pond Pavilion

Introduction

THE CITY OF Kyoto, which became the capital of Japan in 794, was laid out in the form of a neat rectangle in imitation of the Chinese city of Ch'ang-an, capital of the T'ang dynasty, with the imperial palace in the north and a broad thoroughfare, Suzaku-ōji or the Avenue of the Vermilion Bird, running south from the palace gate and dividing the city into eastern and western sectors. To make room for the new city, the course of the Kamo River, which had originally cut through the center of the site, was shifted to the east, so that it ran south along the edge of the eastern sector. In spite of government measures designed to make the citizens dispose themselves with appropriate symmetry on either side of the central avenue, the western sector seems for various reasons to have been unpopular from the first and, as will be seen, grew increasingly deserted through the years. In addition, because the Kamo had been forcibly shifted out of its natural course, and also perhaps because the aristocracy were cutting down trees to build estates along the upper reaches of the river and its tributaries, the city was troubled by frequent floods. The following piece touches upon these problems that beset the city—as well as that of the urban sprawl that was developing in the eastern and northern suburbs and depriving the citizens of their customary recreational areas—before settling down to a description of the author's own home and the spiritual peace he found there.

The author, Yoshishige no Yasutane, was the son of a Kyoto family that specialized in *onyōdō*-style divination and geomancy, but he himself pursued the study of Chinese history and literature. In time he passed the government examination in Chinese studies and held a succession of official posts, culminating in that of secretary in the Nakatsukasa-shō or Ministry of Central Affairs. In 986, after his son had reached the age of maturity, he retired from secular life and became a Buddhist monk. He died in 997. In addition to the piece translated here, he wrote poetry in Japanese and compiled a work entitled *Nihon ōjō gokuraku ki* containing biographies of persons ideas characteristic of the educated class of the time.

The text of the *Record of the Pond Pavilion* is preserved in chapter twelve of the *Honchō monzui*.

Record of the Pond Pavilion

by Yoshishige no Yasutane

FOR THE PAST twenty years and more I have observed the situation throughout the eastern and western sections of the capital. In the western part of the capital the houses have become fewer and fewer till now it's almost a deserted wasteland. People move out of the area but no one moves in; houses fall to ruin but no new ones are ever built. Those who don't have any other place to move to, or who aren't ashamed to be poor and lowly, live there, or people who enjoy a life of obscurity or are hiding out, who ought to return to their native mountains or countryside but don't. But anyone who hopes to pile up a fortune or whose heart is set on rushing around on business wouldn't be able to stand living there even for a day.

In years past there was one mansion there, with painted halls and vermilion doors, groves of bamboo and trees, rocks and fountains—a spot so superb it was like a different world. But the owner was sent into exile because of some affair,[1] and fire broke out and burned the buildings down. There were thirty or forty families of retainers living nearby, but one after another they moved away. Later the owner of the house returned, but he never tried to rebuild; and though he had many sons and grandsons, they didn't remain in the area for long. Thorns and brambles grew till they covered the gate, and foxes and raccoon dogs dug their burrows there in peace. From all this it is clear that it is Heaven that is destroying the western sector and no fault of men.

In the eastern sector of the capital, particularly in the area northeast and northwest of Shijō, live huge crowds of people, eminent and lowly alike. Towering mansions are lined up gate by gate, hall in sight of hall; little huts have only a wall between them, eaves all but touching. If a neighbor to the east suffers a fire, neighbors to the west seldom escape being burned out; if robbers attack the house to the south, the house to the north can't avoid the shower of stray arrows. One branch of a family living south of the avenue is poor, another branch north of the avenue is rich, and though rich relatives may have no special virtue to boast of, poor relatives still must suffer shame. Then there are the humble folk who live in the shadow of some powerful family: their roof is broken but they don't dare thatch it, their wall collapses but they don't dare build it up again; happy, they can't open their mouths and give a loud laugh; grieving, they can't lift up their voices and wail; coming and going always in fear, hearts and minds never at rest, they're like little sparrows in the presence of hawks and falcons. And how much worse when some great mansion is first built and then begins bit by bit to broaden its gates and doors, swallowing up the little huts all around. Then how many of the poor people have occasion to complain, like sons forced to leave the land of their father and mother, like officials of paradise banished to the dusty world of mortals. In farmer constructing embankments along the river and leading water into his paddies. But year after year now there have been floods, the river overflowing and breaking down the levies; and officials charged with keeping the river in check who yesterday boasted of their achievements today leave the breaks sitting as they are. Do they expect the citizens of the capital to turn into fish?

I have privately checked into the regulations and find that in the area west of the Kamo, only the Sūshin-in is permitted to have rice fields; in all other cases they are strictly prohibited because of the danger of flood damage.[2] Moreover, the area east of the river and the northern fields represent two of the four suburbs of the capital, where the Son of Heaven goes to greet the seasons or to enjoy an outing.

If people take it on themselves to build houses there or start growing things, why don't the authorities prohibit and put a stop to it? What about the ordinary citizens who would like to stroll about and amuse themselves? Summer days when people want to enjoy the cool, they find there are no more banks where they can fish for little ayu trout; in the autumn breeze when gentlemen want to go off hunting, they find there are no more fields where they can loose their young falcons. Season by season people scramble to move out of the city, and day by day the area within the capital becomes more deserted, until the wards in the southern section are turned into a vast wilderness of weeds, where only "the ears of grain droop down."[3] Leaving the rich and fertile lands, people go off to barren and stony ground. Is

Heaven causing this as well, or is it the madness of men themselves?

Originally I had no house of my own but stayed in someone else's house at the Jōtō Gate. Constantly aware of the disadvantages of such an arrangement, I decided I didn't want to live there forever, and in fact, even if I had wanted to, it would have been impossible. Estimating that I could buy two or three *se*[4] of land for ten million cash, I finally chose a barren plot north of Rokujō, where I put up a wall on four sides and constructed a gate. I selected the kind of out-of-the-way spot that Prime Minister Hsiao would have approved of, and at the same time aimed for the clean, spacious grounds of Chung-ch'ang T'ung.[5] In all, my land measures some ten or more *se*. Where the ground is high I made a little artificial hill, in the sunken part I dug a small pond. West of the pond I built a small hall to house the Buddha Amida, east of the pond I put up a little building to hold my books, and north of the pond I constructed a low house for my wife and children. In general the buildings cover four tenths of the area, the pond three ninths, the vegetable garden two eighths, and the water-parsley patch one seventh.[6] In addition I have an island with green pines, a beach of white sand, red carp, white herons, a little bridge, and a little boat. Everything I've loved all my life is to be found here. In particular I have the willows on the eastern bank, in spring misty and lithe; in summer the bamboos by the northern door, clear breezes rustling through them; in fall the moon in the western window, bright enough to read a book by; and in winter

the sunlight by the southern eaves, just right for warming my back.

So, after five decades in the world, I've at last managed to acquire a little house, like a snail at peace in his shell, like a louse happy in the seam of a garment. The quail nests in the small branches and does not yearn for the great forest of Teng; the frog lives in his crooked well and knows nothing of the vastness of the sweeping seas. Though as master of the house I hold office at the foot of the pillar, in my heart it's as though I dwelt among the mountains.[7] Position and title I leave up to fate, for the workings of Heaven govern all things alike. Heaven and earth will decide if I live a long life or a short one—like Confucius, I've been praying for a long time now.[8] I do not envy the man who soars like a phoenix on the wind, nor the man who hides like a leopard in the mists. I have no wish to bend my knee and crook my back in efforts to win favor with great lords and high officials, but neither do I wish to shun the words and faces of others and bury myself away in some remote mountain or dark valley. During such time as I am at court, I apply myself to the business of the sovereign; once home, my thoughts turn always to the service of the Buddha. When I go abroad I don my grass-green official robe, and though my post is a minor one, I enjoy a certain measure of honor. At home I wear white hemp garments, warmer than spring, purer than the snow. After washing my hands and rinsing my mouth, I ascend the western hall, call on the Buddha Amida, and recite *The Lotus Sutra*. When my supper is done, I enter the eastern literature, it would be better if we had no teachers. If in being a friend one thinks only of power and profit and cares nothing about the frank exchange of opinions, it would be better if we had no friends. So I close my gate, shut my door, and hum poems and sing songs by myself. When I feel the desire for something more, my boys and I climb into the little boat, thump the gunwale, and rattle the oars. If I have some free time left over, I call the groom and we go out to the vegetable garden to pour on water and spread manure. I love my house—other things I know nothing about.

Since the Ōwa era [961–964], people of the time have taken a fancy to building luxurious mansions and high-roofed halls, even going so far as to have the tops of the pillars carved in the shapes of mountains and duckweed designs incised on the supports of the roof beam.[10] But though the expenditure runs into many millions in cash, they manage to live there barely two or three years. People in old times used to say, "The builder doesn't get to live in what he builds"—how right they were. Now that I am well along in years, I've finally managed to construct a little house, but when I consider it in the light of my actual needs, even *it* seems somewhat too extravagant and grand. Above, I fear the anger of Heaven; below, I am ashamed in the eyes of men. I'm like a traveler who's found an inn along the road, an old silkworm who's made himself a solitary cocoon. How long will I be able to live here?

Ah, when the wise man builds a house, he

causes no expense to the people, no trouble to the spirits. He uses benevolence and righteousness for his ridgepole and beam, ritual and law for his pillar and base stone, truth and virtue for a gate and door, mercy and love for a wall and hedge. Devotion to frugality is his family business, the piling up of goodness his family fortune. When one has such a house to live in, no fire can consume it, no wind topple it, no misfortune come to threaten it, no disaster happen its way. No god or spirit can peer inside it, no thief or bandit can invade. The family who lives there will naturally grow rich, the master will enjoy long life, and office and rank will be with it forever, to be handed down to sons and grandsons. How can one fail, then to exercise caution?

NOTES

1. Minamoto no Takaakira, a high official who in 969 was demoted and assigned to a post in the Dazaifu in Kyushu; he was allowed to return to Kyoto in 972.
2. The Sūshin-in or Cloister for Honoring Relatives, a home for indigent females of the Fujiwara clan founded by a member of the family in 860, was situated in a low-lying area at Gojō Kyōgoku. The regulations that Yasutane refers to prohibited the construction of rice paddies along both the east and west banks of the Kamo.
3. Reference to a poem in the *Shih chi,* "Hereditary House of Sung," which describes the desolate appearance of the former capital of the Yin dynasty.

4. One *se* is approximately equal to one are, 100 square meters or 119.60 square yards.

5. References to the estates of the Chinese statesmen Hsiao Ho of the second century BCE and Chung-ch'ang T'ung of the second century CE.

6. Yasutane's figures clearly aim more at verbal neatness than mathematical accuracy.

7. At this time Yasutane held the post of *naiki* or secretary in the Nakatsukasa-shō, a bureau of the government that handled imperial edicts, petitions, and other documents. "Clerk at the foot of the pillar" was the Chinese term for such a secretary.

8. When Confucius fell ill, one of his disciples asked to be allowed to pray for him, but Confucius replied, "I've been praying for a long time now." *Analects* VII, 34.

9. Emperor Wen reigned from 179 to 157 BCE; Po Lo-t'ien was the polite name for Po Chü-i (772–846), whose poems were greatly admired in Japan and whose prose pieces in fact provided

the model for the present work by Yasutane; the Seven Sages of the Bamboo Grove were a group of Chinese philosopher-poets of the late third century who gathered in a bamboo grove near the capital to drink, play the *ch'in*, and discuss philosophy.

10. The latter part of the sentence is a conventional Chinese expression indicating architectural extravagance and should not necessarily be taken literally.

Record of the
Ten-Foot-Square Hut

⌇

Kamo no Chōmei, who probably lived from 1153 to 1216, was born into a Kyoto family whose male members held a hereditary position as priests of the Kamo Shrine, one of the principal Shinto shrines of the capital. But although Chōmei's father died when Chōmei was in his twenties, Chōmei himself was never permitted to succeed him as a priest of the shrine, a fact that apparently caused him considerable bitterness. Instead he devoted his energies to music—he was particularly distinguished as a player of the *biwa* or lute—and the writing of poetry in Japanese, and he gained a degree of recognition in court circles, some twenty-five of his poems being included in imperially sponsored anthologies. But frustration and disappointment seemed to dog him, and around the age of fifty, having no wife or family to detain him, he renounced the secular world and became a Buddhist monk. His life in the years thereafter is described in the piece that follows.

After retiring from the world, he wrote a work on Japanese poetry and put together a collection of Buddhist exemplary tales, but it is the *Hōjōki* that has won him a place of prime importance in Japanese letters.

Chōmei lived in a time of political and social upheaval, when the two great warrior clans, the Taira and the Minamoto, were contending for dominance of the court and the nation. In addition, natural disasters such as earthquakes and famines added to the distress of the time. The Minamotos eventually emerged victorious, in 1185 wiping out the last of their rivals and founding a shogunate, or military government, in Kamakura, an event that marks the close of the Heian period and the start of a new era in Japanese history and culture.

Another factor that served to deepen the air of unease and pessimism pervading the age was the concept of *mappō* or the End of the Law. According to Buddhist belief, though the Law, or doctrinal teaching of a buddha, may flourish for many centuries after his passing, it is destined in time to decline and fade into ineffectuality. When that fateful era, known as the End of the Law, arrives, evil and disorder will prevail and it will be all but impossible for men and women to gain enlightenment through their own efforts. Japanese Buddhists, reckoning the time that had elapsed since the death of Shakyamuni Buddha, calculated that such an era of *mappō* had begun with the year 1052, a century before Chōmei's birth.

In Chōmei's time it was widely believed that in such an age of moral decline, the only hope for salvation lay in faith in the Buddha Amida, who was said to have taken a vow to welcome all those who sincerely called upon his name to his Pure Land, or Western Paradise. We have already seen reference to the Buddha Amida in the *Record of the Pond Pavilion* by Yoshishige no Yasutane, who was in fact a leader in the early Pure Land or Amidist movement. By the close of the Heian period, when Chōmei lived, devotion to Amida and the practice of the *nembutsu*, the ritual invocation of Amida's name, had become widespread in many sectors of Japanese society. Chōmei, as we will see, was a devout follower of the Amidist faith.

After a famous prefatory passage that muses on the inevitable impermanence of both human beings and the houses they inhabit, Chōmei in his *Record* turns to a description of a series of natural calamities and human disasters that he witnessed in his younger years and that impressed upon him the ephemeral nature of this world. He then alludes to the personal failures and frustrations that increased his longing for religious seclusion, and relates how he retired first to the mountainous area of Ōhara north of Kyoto and then to Mount Hino southeast of the capital, where he built his ten-foot-square hut.[1] He closes with a depiction of his daily activities there and his mental state as he contemplates the approach of death.

The earlier dwellings in this series, those of Po Chü-i and Yoshishige no Yasutane, were fairly ordinary houses, occupied by men who had lifelong careers in government service and enjoyed the comfort and support of family life. Chōmei, by contrast, had no career other than poetry and music, and the religious life in later years, and no wife or family. His dwelling was a much starker affair, and he lived in it all alone. His reclusion is thus more drastic and thoroughgoing than that of his predecessors—one reflecting the somber atmosphere of the era he lived in—and his account of his hut, while drawing upon earlier works in the genre, brings new depths of sensibility to the theme.

Record of the Ten-Foot-Square Hut

by Kamo no Chōmei

THE RIVER FLOWS on unceasingly, but the water is never the same water as before. Bubbles that bob on the surface of the still places disappear one moment, to reappear again the next, but they seldom endure for long. And so it is with the people of this world and with the houses they live in.

In the shining capital, ridgepoles soar side by side, roof tiles vie for height, and the dwellings of eminent and lowly alike seem to endure for generation on generation. But if you inquire into the matter, you find that old houses are in fact very rare. This one burned down a year ago and has just been rebuilt this year; that great mansion fell into ruin, to be replaced by smaller houses. And it is the same with the people who live in them. The sites are unchanged; the people occupying them are many. But of those I used to know, hardly one or two out of twenty or thirty remain. One dies in the morning, another is born at evening—they come and go like froth on the water.

These persons who are born and die—no one knows where they come from or where they go. And these dwellings of a moment—no one knows why their owners fret their minds so over them or are so anxious to make them pleasing to the eye. For both owner and dwelling are doomed to impermanence, no different from the dew on the morning glory.

the northwest. Eventually it spread to the Suzaku Gate of the palace, the hall of state, the imperial university, and the Ministry of the Interior, and in one night all were reduced to ashes. The fire started, it seems, around the intersection of Higuchi and Tominokōji streets, originating in a makeshift shelter where some dancers were putting up for the night.

Because the wind kept shifting direction, the fire spread out fanlike till it covered a wider and wider area. Even houses distant from it were choked with smoke, while everything nearby was enveloped in seething flames. Ashes whirled up into the sky, where they caught the light from the flames, turning the whole sky crimson. Masses of flame, torn by the wind, seemed to fly through the air, leaping whole blocks of the city in their onward march. How could anyone caught in the midst hope to survive? Some, overcome by smoke, sank to the ground, while others were wreathed in sheets of flame and died instantly. Even those who somehow escaped with their lives had no time to rescue their belongings. Thus countless family treasures and precious objects, costing who knows how much, were utterly destroyed.

Sixteen mansions of the nobility were consumed by the fire, to say nothing of untold numbers of other dwellings. Fully one third of the capital was destroyed; several thousand men and women perished, and no one knows how many horses, oxen, and other creatures.

Senseless as all human undertakings are, what could be more foolish than to exhaust one's wealth and burden oneself with worries

by building a house in as perilous a spot as the capital?

The Whirlwind of the Jishō Era

Another time, around the fourth month of the fourth year of the Jishō era [1180], a huge whirlwind sprang up from around the intersection of Nakamikado and Kyōgoku streets and raced down to the Rokujō area. Within the three or four blocks that bore the brunt of its fury, not a single house, big or small, escaped damage. Some were completely flattened, others were stripped down to the bare beams and uprights. Gates were lifted bodily by the wind and deposited four or five blocks away; fences were blown to pieces so that one lot opened directly onto its neighbor. The furnishings and possessions inside the houses were likewise tossed into the sky, and cedar thatching and shingles from the roofs whirled about like dry leaves in a winter wind. Dust rose in a smoke-like pall, making it impossible to see anything, and the roar was so deafening it drowned out all speech. Even the fierce winds that blow evil-doers into hell could not be more terrible, it seemed.

Not only did houses suffer damage, but countless persons who endeavored to clear the wreckage and make repairs were injured or crippled. Later the wind moved off in a south-southwesterly direction, inflicting further suffering on many persons in that area. Whirl-winds occur often enough, people said, but surely this was no ordinary event, and they began to suspect it was in fact some sort of portent of dire things to come.

The Moving of the Capital

Then, in the sixth month of this same fourth year of the Jishō era, the capital was suddenly moved, a totally unexpected occurrence. I have heard that the capital was established at its present site over four hundred years ago, in the reign of Emperor Saga.[2] Without some compelling reason, the location of the capital should never be shifted in such a capricious fashion, and it was quite natural that people of the time felt worried and distressed by the move.

Protest proved fruitless, however, and from

the emperor, his ministers of state, and the court nobles on down, all were obliged to move. No one who served in any sort of government post stayed in the old capital. Everyone who had any thought of gaining rank or employment at court or hoped to profit from imperial favor prepared to move at the earliest possible date. Only those who had missed their chance, who had been shunted aside by the world and had no prospects for advancement, remained behind, brooding on their fate. Dwellings that had formerly vied for grandeur now daily fell into greater disrepair. Houses were dismantled and floated down the Yodo River, the grounds where they had stood reverting to farmland. People changed their tastes, now prizing horses and saddles and no longer riding in ox-drawn carts. All longed to

be a portent of troubled times ahead, and in fact the situation grew more unsettled with each passing day, until people could find no way to allay their fears. And their anxiety was not unfounded, for eventually, in the winter of the same year, the capital was shifted back to its former site. But as for the houses that had been dismantled, it was of course impossible to restore them all to their original condition.

I have heard it said that the sage rulers of antiquity governed the nation with compassion. Their palaces were roofed with mere thatch, left untrimmed at the eaves, and when they saw that little smoke rose from the cooking fires of the people, they excused them from even the light tribute that was ordinarily required.[5] All this they did because they pitied the people and wished to ease their lot. We have only to compare such ways with those in use today to see the difference.

The Famine of the Yōwa Era

Again, sometime around the Yōwa era [1181–82]—it is so long ago I do not recall exactly—there was a dreadful drought and famine that lasted for two years. Spring and summer brought drought, autumn was marked by typhoons and floods, one misfortune followed another so that none of the various types of grain ripened properly. Spring saw the plowing, summer the planting, but autumn witnessed no bustling harvest, winter no storing away. As a result, the people in the different provinces either abandoned their lands and migrated to other regions or left their homes and went to live in the mountains.[6] Prayer services were initiated and special Buddhist rites carried out, but they produced no results whatsoever.

It was customary for the capital to depend on the countryside for all its needs, and once supplies of provisions ceased to come in, the inhabitants found it impossible to continue to live in their usual style. In desperation they brought out one after another of their various treasures, asking so little for them that they were all but throwing them away, but even then they could find no buyers. On the rare occasions when a transaction was arranged, gold counted for little, while grain was the prized item. Beggars lined the roadside, the sound of their pitiful cries dinning in one's ears.

So the first year somehow came to an end,

and it was expected that the new year would bring a return to normalcy. But instead epidemics broke out, adding to the suffering, and relief seemed nowhere in sight. People were now dying of hunger, and each day their plight worsened; they were like fish trapped in shallow water. It reached the point where persons of quality, dressed in their fine hats and leggings, did nothing but go from house to house begging food. Many were overcome by exhaustion and despair in the midst of their ploddings, sinking to the ground where they were. Beside the walls of buildings and along the roads the bodies of those who had starved to death were beyond count. Since nothing was done to remove them, the stench soon filled the city, and the sight of them as they decayed was often too ghastly to look at. The riverbed of defilement and evil to be witness to such heartless acts!

It was particularly pitiful to see how, in the case of husbands and wives who could not bear to be separated, whichever of the pair was most fervent in devotion was always the first to die. This was because, heedless of personal concerns, he or she thought only of the other party, and on the rare occasions when food was to be had would insist that the other one have it. In the case of parents and children, the parents invariably died first. Sometimes a little child, unaware that its mother was dead, would continue to lie beside her, suckling her breast.

Ryūgyō Hōin of Ninna-ji temple, deeply grieved at the vast number of the dying, would write the Sanskrit letter *A* on the forehead of

each dead person he encountered, hoping in this way to assist the deceased to gain salvation.[7]

Regarding the number of dead, it has been estimated that during the fourth and fifth months alone, in the area in the capital south from Ichijō to Kujō and east from Suzaku to Kyōgoku,[8] the corpses found along the roads totaled 42,300, and of course many persons died before and after this two-month period. And if all those who died in the riverbed of the Kamo and in Shirakawa, Nishinokyō, and the various other outlying areas are counted in, the number is almost limitless. How much more so, then, if one takes into account the other regions and provinces of the country!

I have heard that in the reign of Emperor Sutoku, around the Chōjō era [1132–34], a similar situation prevailed, though I have no personal experience of that time. But the dismal events described here I witnessed with my own eyes.

The Great Earthquake of the Genryaku Era [1184–85]

I believe it was around the same time that a great earthquake occurred, quite extraordinary in its magnitude.[9] Mountains tumbled down and blocked the rivers, and the sea seemed to tip over, swamping the land. The ground cracked open and water spurted up, rocks split apart and crashed into the valleys. Boats rowing along the coast were tossed about on the waves, horses could not keep their footing on the roads.

In the region of the capital there was not a single temple or shrine building anywhere that escaped damage. Some were partially destroyed, others collapsed completely. Clouds of dust and soot rose up like billowing smoke, and the roar made by the quaking of the earth and the houses crashing down sounded exactly like thunder. If people remained inside their houses, they were in danger of being crushed, but if they rushed outdoors, the earth opened under them. Without wings, they could hardly fly up into the sky; not being dragons, they were powerless to mount the clouds. I could not help feeling that, among all the frightening things, there is none more frightening than an earthquake.

The violent trembling of the earth ceased after a short while, but the aftereffects continued for quite a time. Not a single day passed without twenty or thirty tremors of the kind that would ordinarily cause great alarm. Only after ten or twelve days had passed did the tremors begin to decrease in frequency, first four or five a day, then two or three, then one every other day or one every two or three days. In all, the aftershocks lasted for some three months.

Of the four great elements, it is ordinarily water, fire, and wind that harm us, while the earth poses no great danger. True, in the Saikō era long ago, there was a great earthquake that wreaked various kinds of havoc, causing the head of the Buddha of Tōdai-ji Temple to fall off.[10] But it could hardly compare to the one I have been describing. At the time of the earlier quake, people all spoke of how fleeting and untrustworthy this world is and for a time appeared to mend their evil ways. But then the days and months went by, and after a year had passed no one any longer even mentioned the event.

The Difficulties of Life in This World

Thus, as we have seen, the world as a whole is a hard place to live in, and both we and our dwellings are precarious and uncertain things. Moreover, in countless instances we encounter further perplexities because of the place we live or our station in life.

If a person of insignificant social standing lives by the gate of some great and influential family, in times of profoundest happiness he does not venture to rejoice too openly, and when sorrows oppress him, he cannot lift up his voice and wail. Never at ease in his comings and goings, timid and fearful each waking moment, he is like a sparrow drawing near to the falcon's nest.

If a poor man lives next door to wealthy people, morning and evening he will feel ashamed of his shabby appearance, going in and out with a self-effacing air. When he observes how his family and servants are filled with envy, or notes the haughty and thoughtless attitude of his rich neighbors, he will be constantly vexed in mind and never content for a moment.

If one lives cramped in a narrow lot, when a fire breaks out nearby one will never escape disaster. And if one lives far out in the country, one has all the inconvenience of traveling back and forth to the city and will be much troubled by thieves.

Possessing power, a man is filled with greed and desire; lacking supporters, he is an object of contempt. Riches bring manifold fears, poverty finds one seething with discontent. Depend upon others and you become their creature; have dependents of your own to look out for and love and obligation ensnare you. If you abide by the world's ways, you suffer the loss of freedom; if you flout them, you are looked on as mad. What place can you live, what activities can you pursue, in order to ensure a haven for your body and bring even a moment of peace to your mind?

Retiring to the Hills of Ōhara

I inherited the house of my paternal grandmother and lived in it for many years. Later,

however, circumstances deprived me of my usual means of support, and though the house held countless memories for me, I was unable to stay there any longer.[11] So when I was something over thirty, I decided to build a little domicile of my own. It was only about one tenth the size of my former dwelling—big enough to live in, though in no way elaborate. It had a mud wall of sorts to enclose it, but I could not afford a proper gate. Using bamboo for posts, I rigged a shed to house the carriage. Whenever it snowed or the wind blew hard, I couldn't help feeling apprehensive. As it stood near the riverbed of the Kamo, there was always the danger of flooding, and I worried a lot about robbers.

For thirty-some years I put up with a world that never seemed to go right, my mind always in turmoil. During that time I met with numerous disappointments and frustrations, and came to realize that I was born to be unlucky. So, in the spring of my fiftieth year, I abandoned secular life, turning my back on the world. Since I had no wife or family to begin with, severing connections was not all that difficult. With no official post or stipend, what was there to cling to? The following five years I spent among the clouds of the Ōhara hills, though I have little to show for it.[12]

Quiet Days on Mount Hino

Now that I've reached the age of sixty, when life fades as quickly as dew, I've put together a lodging for my final days. I'm like a traveler who prepares shelter for one night, or an aging silkworm spinning its cocoon. The size is not even one hundredth that of the house where I lived in middle age. You might say that, as my years have grown in number, my houses have gotten smaller and smaller.

My present place is quite unlike any ordinary dwelling. It measures only ten feet square and less than seven feet in height. Since I never thought of it as a permanent residence, I did not divine to see whether the site was auspicious or not. It has a dirt foundation, a simple roof of thatch, and the joints are held together with metal fastenings. This is so that, if I decide I don't like the spot, I can easily move it. It would be no trouble at all to take it apart and put it together again. Two carts would hold it all, with no other expense than the labor to pull the carts.

Since I came here to hide my traces in the depth of Mount Hino, on the east side of my hut I have extended the eaves out three feet so as to provide a place for firewood and cooking. On the south I constructed a bamboo verandah, with a shelf for vases and other Buddhist articles at the western end. The north side I blocked off with a partition, and adorned it with an image of Amida, the bodhisattva Fugen by his side; a copy of *The Lotus Sutra* is placed in front of them.[13] Along the east edge of the room I've spread soft fern fronds to make a place to sleep at night. In the southwest corner I put up a hanging shelf of bamboo with three leather-covered boxes on it. These are for my books on Japanese poetry and music and for selections from the Buddhist writings such as the *Ōjōyōshū* [*Essentials of Salvation*].[14] Beside them stand my koto and my *biwa*.[15] The koto is the collapsible kind, and the *biwa* has a neck that can be detached. Such is the layout of this little temporary dwelling of mine.

As to my surroundings, south of my hut I have rigged a bamboo pipe that feeds water into a rocky basin I have fashioned. Since there are plenty of forest trees close by, I have no trouble gathering whatever brushwood I need.

This part of the mountain is called Toyama or Outer Hill. The trails are buried in creepers, the valleys dense with vegetation. But I have a clear view to the west, which is some aid to my meditations.[16] In spring I look out on trailing boughs of wisteria, shimmering in the west like

purple clouds.[17] In summer I hear the cuckoo, and with each call he promises to guide me on the road of death.[18] In autumn the cicada's cry fills my ears, and he seems to be lamenting this empty shell of a world. In winter I watch the snows pile up and melt away again, like the sins and impediments in our lives.

When I tire of intoning the *nembutsu*[19] or am not in the mood to recite sutras, I simply give myself a rest and neglect my devotions. There's no one to stop me and no one to feel ashamed on my account. Though I've taken no vow of silence, since I live alone I escape creating any bad karma with my tongue. I make no special effort to keep the precepts, but given my surroundings, what occasion would I have to break them?

Some mornings, when I reflect that this life

of mine is as fleeting as the white waves, I go to Okanoya to watch the boats, stealing a little of Priest Mansei's manner.[20] Other times, at evening when the wind in the maples sets the leaves to rustling, I think of that scene on the river at Hsün-yang and imitate the ways of Minamoto no Tsunenobu.[21] If I am still in the mood for music, I often play "The Melody of the Autumn Wind," blending it with the sighing of the pines, or perform the piece entitled "The Flowing Fountain" to accompany the rippling of the water. I am a very unskilled player, but then my music is not intended to delight the ears of others. I play by myself, sing by myself, and in this way refresh my spirits.

At the foot of the mountain is a rough shack where the caretaker of the mountain lives. He has a little son who now and then comes to visit with me. If I have nothing particular to do, my friend and I go off rambling. He's ten and I'm sixty, so we're far apart in age, but we seem to enjoy the same sort of things.

Sometimes I dig cogon grass sprouts, pick rock-pear berries, or gather basketfuls of cress or tubers of wild taro. Other times I go to the rice fields along the border of the mountain, gathering up fallen ears of rice and weaving them into ornamental wreaths. Or if the weather is fair, I clamber up to the peak and gaze far off in the direction of my old home, or at Mount Kohata, or at the village of Fushimi or Toba or Hatsukashi. A fine scene belongs to no one person, so what harm if I take my fill?[22]

If I don't mind the walk and want to venture farther, I go from one mountain ridge to another, climbing over Charcoal Hill, crossing Kasatori, stopping at the temple at Iwama, or paying my respects at Ishiyama Temple.

Other times I make my way over the fields of Awazu, visiting spots associated with the poet Semimaru, or cross the Tanakami River and search out the grave of Sarumaru.[23] On the way back I look for cherry blossoms or enjoy the autumn leaves, or pick fern shoots and gather nuts, offering some to the Buddha and eating the rest myself.

If the night is still, I gaze at the moon in the window, thinking of old friends, or shed tears at the plaintive wail of the monkeys. Fireflies in the clumps of grass might be taken for the distant flares of fishermen on Maki Island,[24] and showers at dawn sound just like tree leaves blowing in a storm. When I hear the cry of the pheasant, I wonder if it is not the voice of my father or mother, and when I see how friendly the deer from the hilltop have become, I realize how far removed I am from the outside world.[25]

Sometimes I stir up the buried embers of the fire, making them my companion in an old man's wakeful night, or I delight in the voice of the owl, since there is nothing fearful about this mountain.[26] Each season in the mountain brings an endless succession of sights. If I find it so, how much more would a person of truly deep feeling and understanding!

When I first came here to live, I in fact expected to stay only a short while, yet now five years have passed. My "temporary dwelling" has become an old home of sorts, the area under the eaves heaped with decaying leaves, the foundation overgrown with moss. News sometimes reaches me from the capital, and since retiring to this mountain I have learned of the passing of numerous persons of high rank; and how many others of lesser station have died in that time it is impossible to tell. How many, too, are the houses that have been destroyed in the fires that break out from time to time! Only this temporary dwelling of mine has remained tranquil and safe from harm.

Small as it is, it provides room enough to sleep at night and to sit in the daytime, all that is needed to accommodate one person. The hermit crab prefers a little shell because he knows the dimensions of his own body. The fish hawk dwells on the crag-bound shore because he fears to be where people are. And I am the same. Knowing my own size and knowing the ways of the world, I crave nothing, chase about after nothing. I desire only a peaceful spot, and delight in being free from care.

When ordinary people build a house, they do not always build it for themselves alone. Sometimes they build it for their wife and children or for the other members of their family and household. Sometimes they build it for their friends or close associates, or even perhaps for their lord or their teacher, for their valuables and possessions, their horses and oxen. But now I have fashioned a house for myself alone, not for anyone else. Why? Because, the times being what they are and I the person I am, I have no one to be a companion, no servant in my employ. If I built a big house, who would occupy it, who would I house there?

In choosing friends, people look first of all for someone who is rich and can benefit them; they don't necessarily care if the person is upright or genuine in feeling. Better to have no friends but musical instruments and the beauties of nature! In the case of servants, they favor a master who is openhanded and rewards them lavishly, and don't care whether he is kind and thoughtful and truly concerned about their welfare. Better to have no servants other than one's own body!

And how do you proceed with such a servant? If something has to be done, you do it yourself. You may get a bit tired, but it's easier than employing another person and having to look out for him. If there's a distance to be walked, you walk it yourself. It may fatigue you, but it's better than fretting over horse and saddle, ox and oxcart.

Now I divide my body into two faculties, hands for servants, feet for a vehicle, and they perform very well for my mind. Because my mind knows when my body is weary, it can rest it at such times and employ it only when it's feeling fit. It never asks too much of the body or grows impatient when energy flags. Moreover, this constant walking and working benefits my health. Why would I want to just rest all the time? It's sinful to burden others. How could it be right to live at the expense of someone else's labor?

Matters of food and clothing I handle in the same way. A robe of wisteria fiber, a quilt of hemp—I use whatever comes to hand to clothe my nakedness. Starwort from the meadow, nuts from the hilltop trees—just so it's enough to keep me alive. Since I don't mingle with others, I never need feel ashamed of my appearance. Since my food supplies are so skimpy, I appreciate them all the more and eat them with relish. I do not relate these pleasures merely to show my spite for the rich but to indicate how the life of one person differs now from what it was in the past.

This threefold world of ours is a creation of the mind.[27] If the mind is not at ease, then the finest horses and elephants, the seven precious substances, all seem worthless, and palaces and pleasure towers hold no allure. But now I find myself loving this lonely dwelling, my one-room hut. I feel ashamed whenever circumstances oblige me to go to the capital and beg for alms. But once back in my mountain, I can only pity those who chase after worldly gain. If people doubt what I say, let them look at the fish and birds. The fish never tire of the water, yet if one is not a fish, one can hardly understand what is in the fish's mind. Birds long only for the forest, but if one is not a bird, one cannot understand why. The same applies to these delights of the quiet life. Without living such a life, how can one comprehend them?

Now my term draws to a close, like a moon nearing the rim of the mountain as it sinks in the sky. Soon I will face the darkness of Sanzu River.[28] What use now in grumbling? The teachings of the Buddha warn us against feelings of attachment. So now it must be wrong for me to love this thatched hut of mine, and

my fondness for quiet and solitude must be a block to my salvation. Why have I wasted precious time in the recital of these useless pleasures?

In the stillness of dawn I go on pondering these truths, and I put this question to myself: You say you've abandoned the world and come to live in the mountain forest so you can discipline your mind and practice the Way. But however much you imitate a saint's appearance, your mind is still steeped in impurity. In your dwelling you presume to copy the ways of the lay believer Pure Name, but in religious attainment you can't even equal Shuddhipanthaka![29] Is this because you let the poverty that is your lot in life distract you, or have vain delusions unbalanced your mind?

At that time my mind could give no answer.

All I could do was call upon my tongue to utter two or three recitations of Amida Buddha's name, ineffectual as they might be, before falling silent.

> *Written in the second year of the Kenryaku era [1212], around the last day of the third month, by the shramana Ren'in in his hut on Toyama.*[30]

NOTES

1. The term for *ten-foot-square* is *hōjō*, "one-*jō*-square," a *jō* being a linear measure equivalent to ten *shaku* or feet. "One *jō* square" is an accurate description of the small hut in which the author spent his last years. At the same time it calls to mind the tiny one-*jō*-square room of the Buddhist sage Vimalakirti, described in the sutra that bears his name, which was yet miraculously able to accommodate a vast multitude of visitors. The sutra, it may be noted, does not mention the exact dimensions of the room. These come from a legend of how a Chinese pilgrim visited India and was shown what were said to be the remains of Vimalakirti's room. Measuring the foundations, he found them to be ten feet square.

2. Chōmei's account is misleading; the capital was established at Heiankyō or Kyoto in 794, in the reign of Emperor Saga's father, Emperor Kammu. In 1180 Taira no Kiyomori, who wielded dictatorial power at the time, moved the capital to Fukuhara in Settsu, the site of the present-day city of Kobe on the Inland Sea.

3. Oxcarts were the mode of travel of the older, courtier, class, while the samurai, or warriors, now rising to prominence, rode horses. The domains of the Taira or Heike clan were in western Japan. Their rivals, the Minamoto clan, out of power at this time, had their base in the north and east.

4. The Log Palace was a rustic-style temporary residence built for Empress Saimei at Asakura in Kyushu in 661, when she was on her way to aid the country of Paekche in Korea.

5. Chōmei is alluding to accounts of the frugal and beneficent ways of certain ancient rulers of China and Japan.

6. Where they could gather nuts and edible wild plants.

7. Ryūgyō (d. 1206) was a high-ranking member of the Buddhist clergy, as the title Hōin indicates. Ninna-ji is a prominent temple situated in the western suburbs of Kyoto. In Esoteric Buddhism, of which Ninna-ji was a major center, the letter *A*, the first letter of the Sanskrit alphabet, symbolizes the underlying truth of the universe, and contemplation of it is believed to ensure attainment of Buddhahood.

8. That is, the densely inhabited eastern half of the city. The western half was at this time largely unpopulated.

9. The earthquake occurred in the seventh month of 1185.

10. The earthquake occurred in 855, the second year of the Saikō era. Tōdai-ji, one of the main temples of Nara, is famous for its giant bronze image of the Buddha Vairochana.

11. Chōmei's family held a hereditary post as Shinto

priests of the Kamo Shrine in Kyoto, but after his father died when Chōmei was in his twenties, the post was withdrawn.

12. Chōmei is implying that, despite the fact that he took up the religious life, he failed to gain the kind of enlightenment that might be expected.

13. The bodhisattva Samantabhadra or Fugen is often depicted acting as an attendant to the Buddha Amida.

14. A work by the Japanese priest Genshin (942–1017). It is made up of excerpts from various Buddhist scriptures and deals in particular with devotion to the Buddha Amida and the goal of rebirth in Amida's Pure Land, or Western Paradise.

15. The koto, the Japanese version of the Chinese *ch'in*, is a stringed instrument that is played in a horizontal position. The *biwa*, called *p'i-p'a* in Chinese, is a lutelike instrument with a long neck.

16. Meditations on Amida's Western Paradise.

17. The purple clouds that accompany Amida when he appears in the sky to welcome a dying person to his Pure Land.

18. The cuckoo, the bird of the nether world, is believed to act as a guide to the souls of the dead.

19. The ritual invocation of Amida's name, NAMU AMIDA BUTSU.

20. Okanoya is a spot on the Uji River near Chōmei's hut. Chōmei means that at times he writes poetry like the Buddhist priest Mansei (early eighth century). He is alluding to Mansei's famous poem, preserved in chapter twenty of the anthology *Shūishū*, which reads:

> What to compare this world to?
> White waves
> in the wake of a boat
> rowing off
> into the dawn.

21. Chōmei is alluding to the poem entitled "Song

of the Lute" by the Chinese poet Po Chü-i (772–846), written when the poet was in exile in Hsün-yang on the Yangtze. The poem describes a woman playing a *p'i-p'a* or *biwa* in a boat on the river. Minamoto no Tsunenobu (1016–1097) was a famous poet and player of the *biwa*.

22. An allusion to the second couplet in Po Chü-i's four-line poem entitled "Visiting Yün-chü Temple":

> Fine scenes have never had any fixed owner.
> Mountains belong to people who love mountains.

23. Semimaru, a poet of the Heian period, lived in a hut in the area around the southern end of Lake Biwa that Chōmei is describing. Sarumaru was a poet of the early Heian period.

24. An island in the nearby Uji River. The fishermen use flares to attract the fish.

25. The first part of the sentence alludes to a poem on the pheasant by the Buddhist priest Gyōgi (668–749). The second part alludes to the following poem by the poet-priest Saigyō (1118–1190):

> So remote the mountains,
> deer fearless enough
> to come right up close
> tell me how far I am
> from the outside world.

26. An allusion to another poem in the same series by Saigyō:

> So remote the mountains,
> no friendly birds
> chirping close by—
> only the fearful
> voice of the owl.

27. In Buddhist thought the threefold world, made up of the world of desire, the world of form,

and the world of formlessness, constitutes the realm of ordinary unenlightened beings. It is said to be the creation of the mind because it is the mind that invests the world with value, arbitrarily decreeing that certain phenomena are desirable or undesirable, beautiful or ugly, good or bad, and so forth.

28. The swift-flowing river of the dark underworld that the dead must cross before they go on to their next existence.

29. The lay believer Pure Name is Vimalakirti, whose name in Sanskrit means "pure name"; see note 1 above. Shurihandoku or Shuddhipanthaka was the dullest and least apt of Shakyamuni Buddha's disciples.

30. *Sōmon* or *shramana* is a term for a Buddhist monk. Ren'in, which means "heir of the lotus," is Chōmei's religious name.

Record of the Hut of the
Phantom Dwelling

∽

Introduction

THE LAST OF the four huts is that occupied
for a time by the famous Japanese haiku poet
Matsuo Bashō and described in his *Genjūan no
ki* or *Record of the Hut of the Phantom Dwelling*. The
piece is in *haibun*, a kind of poetic prose style,
and serves as an elaborate headnote to the
haiku with which it concludes. It is the shortest
of the four pieces, perhaps because Bashō occupied his hut for a shorter time than any of
the other *Record* writers, a brief six months in
the latter part of 1690. It is also one of the
sunniest in outlook, perhaps because Bashō
had the good fortune to live in an era of peace

and social stability. His hut was situated on a hill on the southern shore of Lake Biwa east of Kyoto, not many miles from the site of Kamo no Chōmei's ten-foot-square hut, and Bashō mentions several of the same places that Chōmei had.

In his youth Bashō served as page to the son of the feudal lord of his domain, but when his young master died suddenly of illness, Bashō left the service of the family and devoted the rest of his life to poetry. He engaged in religious study and training under a master of the Zen sect and, like Kamo no Chōmei, remained unmarried all his life. In his late years he made a number of journeys around Japan, writing poems and poetic diaries on the places he visited.

Bashō's *Record*, though undoubtedly influenced by the earlier works in the same form by Yoshishige no Yasutane and Kamo no Chōmei, for the most part eschews the kind of social or philosophical commentary included in those works and reverts instead to the highly personal note of the earliest piece in the series, Po Chü-i's, thus in a sense completing the circle and returning the form to its point of origin.

Record of the Hut of the Phantom Dwelling

by Matsuo Bashō

BEYOND ISHIYAMA, with its back to Mount Iwama, is a hill called Kokubuyama— the name, I think, derives from a *kokubunji* or government temple of long ago. If you cross the narrow stream that runs at the foot and climb the slope for three turnings of the road, some two hundred paces each, you come to a shrine of the god Hachiman. The object of worship is a statue of the Buddha Amida. This is the sort of thing that is greatly abhorred by the Yuiitsu school, though I regard it as admirable that, as the Ryōbu assert, the buddhas should dim their light and mingle with the dust in order to benefit the world.[1]

Ordinarily, few worshipers visit the shrine, and it's very solemn and still. Beside it is an abandoned hut with a rush door. Brambles and bamboo grass overgrow the eaves, the roof leaks, the plaster has fallen from the walls, and foxes and raccoon dogs make their den there. It is called the Hut of the Phantom Dwelling. The owner was a monk, an uncle of the warrior Suganuma Kyokusui. It has been eight years since he lived there—nothing remains of him now but his name, Elder of the Phantom Dwelling.

I too gave up city life some ten years ago, and now I'm approaching fifty. I'm like a bagworm that's lost its bag, a snail without its shell. I've tanned my face in the hot sun of Kisakata in Ōu and bruised my heels on the rough beaches of the northern sea, where tall dunes make walking so hard.[2] And now this year here I am drifting by the waves of Lake Biwa. The grebe attaches its floating nest to a single strand of reed, counting on the reed to keep it from washing away in the current. With a similar thought, I mended the thatch on the eaves of the hut, patched up the gaps in the fence, and at the beginning of the fourth month, the first month of summer, moved in for what I thought would be no more than a brief stay. Now, though, I'm beginning to wonder if I'll ever want to leave.

Spring is over, but I can tell it hasn't been gone for long. Azaleas continue in bloom, wild wisteria hangs from the pine trees, and a cuckoo now and then passes by. I even have greetings from the jays and woodpeckers that peck at things, though I don't really mind—in fact, I rather enjoy them. I feel as though my spirit had raced off to China to view the scenery in Wu or Ch'u, or as though I were standing beside the lovely Hsiao and Hsiang rivers or Lake Tung-t'ing. The mountain rises behind me to the southwest, and the nearest houses are a good distance away. Fragrant southern breezes blow down from the mountaintops, and north winds, dampened by the lake, are cool. I have Mount Hie and the tall peak of Hira to look at, and this side of them the pines of Karasaki veiled in mist, as well as a castle, a bridge, and boats fishing on the lake.[3] I hear the voice of the woodsman making his way to Mount Kasatori, and the songs of the seedling

planters in the little rice paddies at the foot of the hill. Fireflies weave through the air in the dusk of evening, clapper rails tap out their notes—there's surely no lack of beautiful scenes. Among them is Mikamiyama, which is shaped rather like Mount Fuji and reminds me of my old house in Musashino, while Mount Tanakami sets me to counting all the poets of ancient times who are associated with it.[4] Other mountains include Bamboo Grass Crest, Thousand Yard Summit, and Skirt Waist. There's Black Ford Village, where the foliage is so dense and dark, and the men who tend their fish weirs, looking exactly as they're described in the *Man'yōshū*.[5] In order to get a better view all around, I've climbed up on the height behind my hut, rigged a platform among the pines, and furnished it with a round room where the Buddha image is kept, there is only a little place designed to store bedding.

An eminent monk of Mount Kōra in Tsukushi, the son of a certain Kai of the Kamo Shrine, recently journeyed to Kyoto, and I got somebody to ask him if he would write a plaque for me. He readily agreed, dipped his brush, and wrote the three characters Gen-jū-an. He sent me the plaque, and I keep it as a memorial of my grass hut. Mountain home, traveler's rest—call it what you will, it's hardly the kind of place where you need any great store of belongings. A cypress-bark hat from Kiso, a sedge rain cape from Koshi—that's all that hang on the post above my pillow. In the daytime I'm once in a while diverted by people who stop to visit. The old man who looks after the shrine or the men from the village come and tell me about the wild boar who's been eating the rice plants, the rabbits that are getting at the bean patches—tales of farm matters that are all quite new to me. And when the sun has begun to sink behind the rim of the hills, I sit quietly in the evening waiting for the moon so I may have my shadow for company, or light a lamp and discuss right and wrong with my silhouette.

But when all has been said, I'm not really the kind who is so completely enamored of solitude that he must hide every trace of himself away in the mountains and wilds. It's just that, troubled by frequent illness and weary of dealing with people, I've come to dislike society. Again and again I think of the mistakes

I've made in my clumsiness over the course of the years. There was a time when I envied those who had government offices or impressive domains, and on another occasion I considered entering the precincts of the Buddha and the teaching rooms of the patriarchs. Instead, I've worn out my body in journeys that are as aimless as the winds and clouds, and expended my feelings on flowers and birds. But somehow I've been able to make a living this way, and so in the end, unskilled and talentless as I am, I give myself wholly to this one concern, poetry. Po Chü-i worked so hard at it that he almost ruined his five vital organs, and Tu Fu grew lean and emaciated because of it. As far as intelligence or the quality of our writings go, I can never compare to such men. And

NOTES

1. In Bashō's time the Buddhist and Shinto religions had become so interfused that it was not uncommon for a Buddhist image to be worshiped in a shrine dedicated to a Shinto deity such as Hachiman. The Yuiitsu school of Shinto strongly opposed such syncretism, but the more common Ryōbu faction looked upon the Shinto deities as avatars of the buddhas—Hachiman was thought to be an avatar of Amida—and saw it as admirable that the buddhas should set aside their dignity and deign to take on the form of local Japanese gods in order to save people.

2. References to the trip to northern Japan that Bashō described in his famous travel diary *Oku no hosomichi* or "Narrow Road to the Interior."

3. Zeze Castle and Seta Bridge, the latter where the Seta River flows out of the south end of Lake Biwa.
4. The mountain is the site of graves or shrines associated with various poets, such as Ki no Tsurayuki (c. 868–c. 946).
5. The *Man'yōshū* (Collection of Myriad Leaves) is the oldest extant anthology of Japanese poetry, compiled late in the eighth century.

SHAMBHALA CENTAUR EDITIONS

are named for a classical modern typeface designed by the eminent American typographer Bruce Rogers. Modeled on a fifteenth-century Roman type, Centaur was originally an exclusive titling font for the Metropolitan Museum of Art, New York. The first book in which it appeared was Maurice de Guérin's *The Centaur*, printed in 1915. Until recently, Centaur type was available only for handset books printed on letterpress. Its elegance and clarity make it the typeface of choice for Shambhala Centaur Editions, which include outstanding classics of the world's literary and spiritual traditions.

(Continued on next page)

PRAYER OF THE HEART
Writings from the *Philokalia*
Compiled by St. Nikodimos of the Holy
Mountain and St. Makarios of Corinth
Translated by G. E. H. Palmer, Philip Sherrard,
and Kallistos Ware

A STRANGER TO HEAVEN AND EARTH
Poems of Anna Akhmatova
Translated by Judith Hemschemeyer

THE TALE OF CUPID AND PSYCHE
by Lucius Apuleius
Translated by Robert Graves

A TOUCH OF GRACE
Songs of Kabir
Translated by Linda Hess and Shukdev Singh